FART PHILOSOP

Silent But Wise

The Subtle Art of Fart-Based Wisdom

Tim Hendy

For permission requests, please contact the publisher at:
wisdom@fart-philosphy.co.uk
fart-philosphy.co.uk
Instagram @fart.philosophy

ISBN: 978-1-0369-2603-8

First Edition: 2025

Introduction

Throughout history, humanity has sought wisdom in the strangest of places—mountaintop monasteries, ancient scrolls, the musings of great philosophers. But what if some of the deepest truths of life have been floating under our noses all along? Welcome to the art and philosophy of flatulence, where every toot carries a lesson, and the winds of wisdom blow freely.

From the crude humor of the common man to the enlightened chuckles of intellectuals, flatus has always held a peculiar place in human culture. Whether in the whispered jokes of schoolchildren or the unfiltered commentary of great minds like Benjamin Franklin, who once penned an essay on the virtues of breaking wind, farting is more than mere bodily function—it is a metaphor for life itself.

This book takes a collection of quotes related to the noble act of passing gas and applies them to real-world wisdom. Whether it's about embracing authenticity, handling awkward situations, or simply learning to let go, fart philosophy offers surprisingly profound insights wrapped in a cloud of humor.

So take a deep breath (or maybe don't), and prepare yourself for an enlightening journey through the philosophy of the fart—because sometimes, the best wisdom is the kind that sneaks up on you when you least expect it.

For my wife who has not only tolerated my farts, but has always understood my reason for farting in the first place and to Sam who's farts were always better than mine.

1.

Better out than in.

Don't bottle up your emotions; it's healthier to let them out.

2.

A silent one can be the deadliest.

Sometimes, the most subtle actions or words have the biggest impact.

3.

If you hold it in too long, it'll only cause you discomfort.

Ignoring your problems won't make them go away; address them before they build up.

4.

Everyone does it, but no one wants to admit it.

We all have flaws and embarrassing moments; don't be ashamed of being human.

5.

The longer you try to hide it, the more obvious it becomes.

Deception often draws more attention than honesty.

6.

Own it, and people will respect you more.

Confidence and honesty go a long way, even in awkward situations.

7.
A well-timed release can clear the air

The right words at the right time can diffuse tension and bring clarity.

8.

If it stinks, at least make it funny.

Life's mishaps are easier to handle with a sense of humour.

9.

Better to let it go naturally than force it out at the wrong time.

Patience is key; don’t rush things before they’re ready.

10.

Those who judge you for it have probably done worse.

Don't worry about criticism from people who have their own flaws.

11.

Sometimes, it's best to step outside and let things pass.

Walking away from a heated situation can be the best solution.

12.

If it lingers, open a window and move on.

Don't dwell on past mistakes; take action and keep going.

13.
A loud one can be shocking, but at least it's honest.

Speaking your mind may surprise people, but honesty is valuable.

14.

It's only embarrassing if you make a big deal out of it.

Confidence can turn an awkward moment into a non-issue.

15.

The most unexpected ones often leave the biggest impression.

Great ideas, like surprises, can come out of nowhere and make an impact.

16.

If it slips out, don't panic—just carry on.

Mistakes happen; it's how you handle them that matters.

17.

Sometimes, a little warning would be appreciated.

Good communication prevents surprises and misunderstandings.

18.

The worst ones come when you least expect them.

Challenges in life often arise when you're least prepared.

19.

It's always funnier when it happens to someone else.

Perspective is everything;
learn to laugh at yourself.

20.

If it happens in a crowded room, share the blame.

Teamwork means sticking together in tough situations.

21.

Some are just hot air with no real impact.

Not everything that sounds important actually is.

22.
You might regret letting it out, but keeping it in is worse.

Speak your truth,
even if it's uncomfortable.

23.

A good one can make everyone laugh and bring people together.

Shared experiences create stronger connections.

24.

If it makes someone run for cover, maybe apologise.

Own up to your mistakes
and make amends.

25.

Don't let one bad moment define you.

Everyone has embarrassing slip-ups; move on.

26.

If it's too loud, just smile and act natural.

Confidence can get you through almost anything.

27.

If people are offended, that's their problem.

You can't please everyone, so don't try too hard.

28.
Sometimes it's better to walk away before people notice.

Knowing when to exit a situation is a valuable skill.

29.

If you try to blame someone else, chances are they'll do the same to you.

Taking responsibility earns respect.

30.

The stink will pass, but the memory might linger.

People may forget what you did, but not how you made them feel.

31.

If you do it confidently, people might think you meant to.

Own your actions, and others will respect you for it.

32.

Some people pretend it never happened, others embrace it with pride.

Attitude makes
all the difference.

33.

It's natural, but that doesn't mean you should do it in an elevator.

There's a time and place for everything.

34.

It's worse when you try too hard and nothing happens.

Forcing things rarely leads to good results.

35.
If you do it too often, people might start avoiding you.

Know when to hold back to maintain good relationships.

36.

It's always funnier when it echoes.

The impact of your words and actions depends on the setting.

37.
The worst ones are often caused by what you've consumed.

Be mindful of what you take in—
physically and mentally.

38.

Some will judge you, but deep down, they've done it too.

People are often guilty of the same things they criticise.

39.

If you pretend it never happened, others might too.

Confidence (or ignorance) can sometimes smooth over a situation.

40.

A well-placed one can break the tension in a room.

The right words at the right time can ease difficult situations.

41.
You'll know who your true friends are by how they react.

Real friends stick with you through embarrassing moments.

42.
If it's really bad, take responsibility and move on.

Owning up to mistakes is better than making excuses.

43.

Sometimes, you just have to let it rip and hope for the best.

Taking risks can be nerve-wracking, but necessary.

44.

If it happens at the wrong time, just laugh it off.

A sense of humour can make any situation better.

45.
It's a relief when it's finally out.

Speaking your mind can feel liberating.

46.

Holding it in too long can make things awkward.

Avoiding tough conversations only makes them harder later.

47.
The buildup is often worse than the actual event.

Fear of failure is usually more daunting than failure itself.

48.

Some are forgettable, others leave a lasting impression.

Not every moment in life is significant, but some are.

49

The smell always gives it away, no matter how hard you try to hide it.

The truth has a way of coming out eventually.

50.
In the right company, it's nothing to be ashamed of.

Surround yourself with people who accept you as you are.

51.

The best ones make people laugh instead of cringe.

Choose your words carefully to create joy rather than discomfort.

52.

If you keep denying it, people will only suspect you more.

Owning your actions is often better than covering them up.

53.

The worst offenders are usually the first to blame.

Hypocrisy is easy to spot.

54.

Sometimes, the quietest ones are the most powerful.

True strength isn't always loud or obvious.

55.
When it happens, just embrace it—there's no turning back.

Once you commit to something,
see it through.

56.

You can always tell when someone is trying to hold one in.

Suppressed emotions or tension are often easy to notice.

57.

It's only truly embarrassing if you make a fuss about it.

Many awkward situations can be smoothed over with confidence.

58.

A little one might go unnoticed, but a big one will be remembered forever.

Small mistakes fade,
but big moments define you.

59.

If people walk away from you, maybe take it as a sign.

Learn from rejection
rather than ignoring it.

60.
Follow through, but not blindly.

The outcome matters
more than the effort.

61.

Some leave a mark long after they've gone.

Your actions and words can have a lasting impact.

62.

If it's unexpected, just act as if nothing happened.

Confidence can make even the most awkward situations manageable.

63.

Sometimes, you just have to step outside and let things settle.

Distance yourself from drama
to gain perspective.

64.

At the end of the day, it's all just a part of life.

Don't take yourself too seriously.

65.
If it's brewing, best to find a private spot.

Some things are best handled discreetly.

66.
What goes in must come out.

Everything has consequences; be mindful of your choices.

67.

If you do it with confidence, people might think it was intentional.

How you carry yourself matters more than what happens.

68.

If people start fanning the air, take the hint.

Learn to read social cues
and act accordingly.

69.

A little warning goes a long way.

Give people a heads-up before dropping unexpected news.

70.

Sometimes, you have to take responsibility for the atmosphere you've created.

Your actions shape your environment.

71.

It's better to ease it out slowly than to force it and regret it.

Take your time
with big decisions.

72.

No matter how much you deny it, the truth always lingers.

Avoiding responsibility won't make a problem disappear.

73.
The bigger the buildup, the bigger the release.

Holding back emotions or ideas too long can lead to explosive results.

74.

Sometimes, all you can do is laugh and move on.

Not everything has to be taken seriously.

75.

If people distance themselves from you, consider what you've put out there.

Your actions and words affect relationships.

76.

If you try to sneak one out, don't be surprised if you get caught.

Deception is rarely as subtle as you think.

77.
You might think it's nothing, but others will definitely notice.

Even small actions
can have big effects.

78.

Some are short and sweet; others linger longer than you'd like.

Not all experiences are equal,
but they all shape you.

79.
You don't always know how bad it is until people react.

Sometimes, we underestimate the impact of our actions.

80.
When in doubt, blame the dog.

While passing the blame may be tempting, honesty is always best.

81.

Trying to cover it up usually makes it worse.

Lies and excuses only add to the problem.

82.
Timing is everything.

A well-placed joke (or action) can make all the difference.

83.

If it makes others laugh, you've turned an awkward moment into a win.

A sense of humour
can save the day.

84.

Sometimes, the only option is to leave the room and start fresh.

Walking away from a bad situation can be the best move.

85.

Don't make a big deal out of it, and neither will anyone else.

Most problems shrink when you don't overreact.

86.
People will forget the noise, but not the smell.

Actions speak louder than words;
people remember impact, not intent.

87.
If it's coming, best to brace yourself and let it happen.

Accept what you can't control
and ride it out.

88.
If it's loud enough, you might as well own it.

Bold actions require
bold ownership.

89.

A change in diet can make all the difference.

Small lifestyle adjustments
can lead to big improvements.

90.

What's funny to you might not be funny to others.

Be aware of
different perspectives.

91.

Don't be the one who stinks up the whole room.

Contribute positively to your environment.

92.

You can pretend it didn't happen, but others will know.

Denying reality
rarely fools anyone.

93.

If you have to apologise, keep it short and sincere.

Owning up to mistakes is important, but don't dwell on them.

94.

Some people will pretend they didn't notice just to be polite.

Kindness often means letting small things slide.

95.

Your reaction matters more than the fart itself.

People remember how you handle situations, not just what happened.

96.

If you must, at least try to make it sound elegant.

There's an art to handling awkward situations with grace.

97.

Never trust one that feels risky.

Sometimes, holding back is the wiser choice.

98.

The best ones bring joy to the people around you.

Share things that
uplift others.

99.
If you do it too often, people will start avoiding you.

Don't overuse anything,
from jokes to favours.

100.
At the end of the day, we're all human.

Everyone makes mistakes,
so don't stress over the little things.

Thanks for reading.

Printed in Dunstable, United Kingdom

71705523R00061